Bryan Johnson:
Life Unveiled –
Navigating Fortune,
Love, and the Quest For
Timeless Youth
By
Kyrie Petra

Table Of Contents

Overview

Within the expansive terrain of Silicon Valley, the meeting point of creativity and entrepreneurship, Bryan Johnson is a remarkable individual whose path surpasses the limits of traditional achievement. "Bryan Johnson: Life Unveiled – Navigating Fortune, Love, and the Quest For Timeless Youth" explores the complex life of a man characterized by unwavering pursuit of the exceptional, ground-breaking endeavors, and unrelenting ambition.

The introduction provides the starting point for readers to enter the mysterious world of Bryan Johnson, providing an overview of the key events and early influences that shaped his extraordinary journey. Johnson was born in Provo, Utah, on August 22, 1977. A combination of personal struggles, an entrepreneurial energy, and an unwavering desire to push limits molded Johnson's early years.

As we set out on this narrative journey, we'll explore the terrain of Johnson's early business endeavors, starting with the establishment of Braintree in 2007—a business that would go on to reinvent online payment systems and cemented his reputation as a tech titan. The reader will follow the development of a youthful business person as they navigate the complex network of ventures, triumphs, and failures that finally led to the establishment of Braintree, a significant turning point in Johnson's remarkable career.

But this biography digs further into Johnson's personal life, including aspects outside of the boardroom as well. His brief affair with actress and content producer Taryn Southern will be discussed in the introduction, which will also set the scene for the turbulent events that take place later in the story. As a story of resiliency, love, and unanticipated obstacles unfolds, the nuances of striking a balance between love, personal goals, and the unwavering pursuit of professional achievement are highlighted.

As the narrative progresses, readers will learn about the versatile entrepreneur's 2016 foundation of Kernel, a company dedicated to solving the mysteries surrounding the human brain, and his journey into the field of neurotechnology. The introduction offers a glimpse into Johnson's always evolving vision, in which the deep desire for longevity and self-improvement blends with technical advancement.

The opening of "Bryan Johnson: Life Unveiled" establishes the tone for a story that transcends the conventions of a biography. It challenges readers to delve into the nuances of a life at the crossroads of love, ambition, and the undiscovered territories of anti-aging endeavors. This biography seeks to reveal the facets of Bryan Johnson's fascinating life by painstaking investigation and personal narrative, providing a nuanced viewpoint on the man behind the headlines and the visionary guiding the development of technology and human potential.

"Background and Early Influences"

In order to fully understand Bryan Johnson's remarkable life tale, one needs to return to the picturesque settings of Provo, Utah, where his narrative is told against the background of lowly beginnings and formative events that would eventually define the outlines of his unwavering determination.

Bryan Johnson was the middle child born on August 22, 1977, into a household consisting of three brothers and a sister. Growing up in Springville, Utah, he experienced the difficulties of a changed family environment due to divorce. Johnson found himself living with his mother and stepfather, a trucking business entrepreneur, when his parents divorced. These early family interactions sowed the seeds of self-reliance that would later become defining characteristics of his character, as well as resilience.

The story takes an interesting turn when we learn about Bryan Johnson's transformational adventure as a 19-year-old Mormon missionary in Ecuador. This crucial event broadened his perspective and made him aware of the nuanced aspects of cultural diversity and the lasting value of interpersonal relationships. The demanding nature of missionary work surely aided in the development of the traits that would eventually define Johnson's entrepreneurial style: flexibility, persistence, and a strong conviction in the transformational potential of experiences.

Johnson's quest of education sent him to Brigham Young University, from where he earned a Bachelor of Arts in International

Studies in 2003. The seeds of business started to sprout during these early years. Johnson's early endeavors, which included a mobile phone sales company, demonstrated his natural aptitude for business and provided funding for his schooling. The spirit of tenacity and ingenuity that characterized his early years established the foundation for a career filled with bold business endeavors.

Bryan Johnson carried on with his studies, graduating in 2007 with a Master of Business Administration (MBA) from the University of Chicago Booth School of Business. This was a critical turning point in his development, giving him the business savvy and strategic ideas that would be useful when he founded Braintree, an endeavor that would propel him to the pinnacles of tech celebrity.

Upon dissecting Bryan Johnson's early inspirations and upbringing, the story reveals a tapestry laced with tenacity, fortitude, and an unwavering quest for perfection. Every phase of his early life offers a prism through which to see the origins of his ambition, from the family struggles of his childhood to the life-changing experiences of missionary work and the demanding intellectual environment of higher study. The scene is set for his entrepreneurial adventure, which will unfold in the next chapters as we explore the rapidly changing fields of technology, business, and the quest for perpetual youth.

Synopsis of Bryan Johnson's Career: A Pioneer in Technology and Other Fields

Nothing less than an expedition across the worlds of technology, business, and the undiscovered potential of humankind characterizes Bryan Johnson's voyage. As we go further into his biography, it becomes clear that Johnson's path is more complex than just a story of commercial victories, characterized by bold vision, cutting-edge technology, and an unwavering pursuit of personal development.

Bryan Johnson was a young businessman with an excellent sense of opportunity when he first started out. Between 1999 and 2003, Johnson founded three firms. These weren't simply business initiatives; they also served as stepping stones for his subsequent rise in the entrepreneurship world. The first of them, which included selling mobile phones, not only helped him pay for his schooling but also taught him important lessons about customer service and business dynamics.

Following these first forays, Johnson shown his tenacity and flexibility when he joined a real estate project and eventually entered the VoIP industry with Inquist. Even while these projects did not turn out to be as successful as planned, they did provide the foundation for the tenacity that would characterize Johnson's style of entrepreneurship: a persistent faith in the promise of invention, despite obstacles.

With the establishment of Braintree in 2007, Johnson's entrepreneurial zeal takes center stage, and the story picks up steam. This endeavor not only thrust him into the public eye but also transformed online payment methods, guaranteeing Braintree's position as one of the fastest-growing businesses. Johnson's reputation as a digital tycoon was cemented in 2012 with the purchase of Venmo, and by September 2013, Braintree was handling an astounding $12 billion in payments a year.

But Bryan Johnson's path goes beyond just achieving financial prosperity. The October 2014 debut of OS Fund, a venture capital business powered by Johnson's own wealth, marks the beginning of a significant chapter. This audacious decision highlights his imaginative ambition of influencing the direction of future innovations, going beyond short-term benefits, and demonstrates his dedication to investing in early-stage scientific and technology enterprises.

The plot takes a fascinating turn in 2016 when Kernel is founded, delving into the complex world of neurotechnology. Johnson's vision explores the deep secrets of the human brain and goes beyond the traditional bounds of technology. Johnson's dedication to extending human potential is shown by Kernel's inventions, which include helmet-like instruments used to analyze brain impulses.

As the story progresses, the focus moves to Johnson's 2021 launch of "Project Blueprint," which is his anti-aging initiative. This ambitious initiative closely monitors biomarkers and incorporates customized health modifications, such as consuming more than 100 supplements every day, in an attempt to unlock the mysteries of perpetual youth. Johnson demonstrates the integration of scientific rigor with a personal drive for self-improvement in his pursuit of longevity and optimum well-being.

The story threads the intricacies of Johnson's personal life in between these scientific and technical endeavors. His situation is further complicated by the turbulent affair he had with Taryn Southern, the legal issues, and the difficult balancing act between his personal and professional obligations.

As we begin this thorough examination of Bryan Johnson's life story, it becomes clear that his story goes well beyond the parameters of conventional business. It is the story of a pioneer who, driven by an unquenchable curiosity and an unyielding faith in human potential, has irrevocably changed the fields of science, technology, and the never-ending search for what lies beyond the sun. The next chapters provide a detailed examination of a life that is fundamentally still an intriguing narrative of invention and self-discovery.

"Chapter One: The Entrepreneurial Genesis"

Chapter One of Bryan Johnson's engrossing journey chronicles the entrepreneurial origin, a time when aspirational seeds are planted in the rich soil of inventiveness and resiliency. The early years of Johnson's childhood were framed by Provo, Utah, and it was in this idyllic setting that the seeds of his entrepreneurial drive were planted.

The story begins with Johnson growing up in Springville, Utah, and negotiating the difficulties of a divorce-impacted household. Bryan Johnson, the middle child of three brothers and a sister, was raised in an environment that required flexibility and inventiveness. These early family difficulties helped to cultivate the resilient mindset that would later characterize his business endeavors.

The tale takes an intriguing turn when Johnson, a 19-year-old Mormon missionary in Ecuador, sets off on a life-changing journey. This crucial event acted as a turning point in his life, reshaping his perspective and imparting ideas about belonging, community, and the lasting power of interpersonal connections. The story is resonant with the echoes of his missionary work, providing insights into the development of traits that would prove crucial in his subsequent endeavors: adaptation, cultural awareness, and a resilient attitude in the face of difficulty.

In terms of education, the chapter takes place against the background of Brigham Young University student Bryan Johnson's quest for knowledge. The early rhythms of Johnson's endeavors, such as the mobile phone startup, are fully absorbed by the reader. In addition to providing funding for his studies, this business venture helped him develop an instinctive grasp of consumer interaction and company dynamics, which would come in very handy in the ensuing chapters.

Johnson's venture into VoIP with Inquist and his involvement in a real estate project give the story a boost. Even if these endeavors did not yield the expected results, they did imprint resilience—a trait that would come to define Bryan Johnson's career—into the story. The spirit of entrepreneurship persisted despite obstacles and kept evolving.

The establishment of Braintree in 2007 was the pinnacle of the entrepreneurial origin. In the first chapter, the reader is swept up in the thrilling dynamics of a rapidly growing firm that would change online payment methods and catapult Bryan Johnson into Silicon Valley stardom. Johnson's rise to prominence as a tech mogul is further cemented by the purchase of Venmo in

2012; as of September 2013, Braintree was handling an astounding $12 billion in payments a year.

The reader is left with a picture of Bryan Johnson on the verge of becoming a well-known entrepreneur as the chapter comes to an end. The first flowers of achievement have sprung from the roots of ambition, which have been nurtured in the soil of family struggles and life-changing events. The adventure of entrepreneurship has started, laying the groundwork for future sections that will elucidate the intricacies of an existence experienced at the nexus of inventiveness, aspiration, and the unrelenting quest for uncharted territory.

"Early Ventures and Lessons"

Within the fabric of Bryan Johnson's remarkable journey, the chapter "Early Ventures and Lessons" stands out as a captivating story that reveals the strands of perseverance, flexibility, and priceless lessons learned from the trial by fire that is entrepreneurship. Between 1999 and 2003, Johnson engaged in a number of business endeavors that not only prepared the way for his eventual triumphs but also served as a blank canvas for the entrepreneurial aspirations and unwavering spirit that would come to define his philosophy of doing business.

The chapter begins with Johnson's early years as a picturesque background, guiding him through the difficulties of changing family relations due to divorce. Johnson was a young, desperate businessman whose early projects served as a way to navigate the challenges of tertiary study as well as a source of income. The first of these endeavors was a company that sold mobile phones, which not only helped Johnson pay for his studies but also served as a blank canvas on which he could sketch the fundamentals of customer interaction and business dynamics.

The story reveals the complexities of Inquist, a VoIP business that Johnson co-founded with three other partners, inside the tapestry of early businesses. This project aimed to integrate Skype and Vonage capabilities via a mix of ambition and creativity. Even though Inquist was eventually closed in 2001, the experience served as a harsh classroom for lessons in flexibility and perseverance. It was a period of disappointments that would later play a significant role in molding Johnson's perspective on entrepreneurship as a difficult but rewarding path.

As Johnson teamed up with his brother and another partner on a $70 million real estate deal, the environment of entrepreneurship kept changing. But like its forerunners, this endeavor ran into difficulties and failed to meet the projected sales targets. The story, broken up by these disappointments, creates a vivid picture of the entrepreneurial journey as a tapestry containing both successes and failures.

The insights gained from these first endeavors went beyond the domains of commercial tactics. They developed into a treasure trove of knowledge on the human aspects of entrepreneurship, including the skill of perseverance, the capacity to change course in the face of difficulty, and the inescapable link between failure and progress. This chapter's depiction of the entrepreneurial environment acts as a morality test and a platform for Bryan Johnson's development as a budding visionary.

As the chapter progresses, the reader is allowed access inside Johnson's head to see the confluence of ambition and realism that characterizes his business philosophy. These early endeavors highlight the early years of a maverick entrepreneur, each one serving as a stepping stone on the path to Braintree and beyond. They provide a foundation for teachings that go beyond the immediate gratification of material gain, molding an outlook that views obstacles as opportunities for development and defeat as a necessary step toward success.

"Early Ventures and Lessons" is really a monument to the tenacity of the entrepreneurial spirit rather than just a section in Bryan Johnson's history. It challenges the reader to walk the path where aspiration meets hardship and, out of the furnace of early endeavors, a leader destined for the pinnacles of the IT industry emerges.

Starting Braintree and Creating a Financial Superpower

In Bryan Johnson's life story, the chapter "Launching Braintree: Building a Financial Empire" is an exciting account of his entrepreneurial spirit, inventiveness, and chutzpah in trying to completely change the banking industry. The reader is swept up in the intoxicating ambiance of Silicon Valley as we dig into this crucial chapter, when Johnson's imaginative soul melds with a zeitgeist of technical advancement.

The chapter opens with a background of Johnson's past endeavors, each serving as a stepping stone that added to his experience crucible. Against this background, Braintree appears—an endeavor that would propel Bryan Johnson into the upper echelons of the IT industry while also revolutionizing online payment systems.

The story gives readers a clear image of the vibrant, opportunity- and challenge-filled business scene in the middle of the 2000s. When Braintree was established in 2007, it was more than simply a business endeavor—it revolutionized the way that internet payments were handled. Johnson's goal went beyond just completing a transaction; it also included streamlining and improving the whole payment infrastructure for online retailers.

The reader is drawn into the strategic nuances of Braintree's debut as the narrative progresses. Johnson's insight and in-depth knowledge of market dynamics allowed the business to establish itself as a major player in the financial technology industry. The purchase of Venmo in 2012, a calculated decision that demonstrated Johnson's ability to identify new market trends, enhanced Braintree's position as a dominant player in the fintech industry.

The reader is guided through key moments in Braintree's explosive growth. The firm processed an astounding $12 billion in payments yearly by September 2013, demonstrating Johnson's skill at managing exponential development. The chapter turns into an account of successes, complete with honors like being 47th and 415th, respectively, on Inc. magazine's list of the

500 fastest-growing businesses in 2011 and 2012.

"Launching Braintree" is a study of Bryan Johnson as a visionary leader, not just a list of his financial accomplishments. The story takes the reader through the layers to show Johnson's business philosophy, which was characterized by measured risks, smart thinking, and unwavering drive. The purchase of Venmo, an app that transformed peer-to-peer payments, is evidence of his ability to foresee changes in the market and put Braintree at the forefront of innovation.

This chapter also serves as evidence of Johnson's encouragement of teamwork. These pages vividly depict the team interactions, the Braintree culture, and Johnson's leadership approach. It tells the story of developing an innovative and exceptional culture in addition to constructing a financial empire.

After following the story of Braintree's growth, the chapter ends with the critical acquisition of the firm by PayPal in September 2013 for an astounding $800 million. This historic occasion not only heralded the end of Braintree's voyage but also the beginning of a new phase in Bryan Johnson's business career.

In Bryan Johnson's life, "Launching Braintree: Building a Financial Empire" represents a climax. This is a phase in which aspiration meets strategic acumen, and innovation serves as the medium of exchange for transforming sectors. The epic story of Bryan Johnson continues as the reader flips the pages, leaving them with a deep respect for the visionary who dared to reinvent how the world functions and build the foundation for future chapters.

Chapter 2: The Balancing Act of Personal and Professional Life Beyond Business

In the complex biography of Bryan Johnson, "Chapter Two: Beyond Business - Personal and Professional Balancing Act" takes the reader inside the private workings of a trailblazing businessman who must strike a careful balance between his personal goals and the demands of a growing professional empire. This chapter is woven together like a tapestry with themes of love, ambition, and the complex interplay between the private and public selves.

This chapter's story begins with the fallout from Braintree's 2013 purchase by PayPal, a momentous event that catapulted Bryan Johnson into the upper echelons of the IT industry. The reader follows Johnson through this turning point in his life, as his professional accomplishments are compared against the subtleties of relationship dynamics and personal contentment.

"Beyond Business" expands to include Johnson's responsibilities as a husband, father, and business owner in addition to his entrepreneurial function. The chapter offers a unique look into the complexities of Johnson's personal life, including juggling the demands of family obligations with the difficulties that come with having a prominent position in the tech sector.

The contrast between the public and private domains is highlighted as Johnson, the visionary businessman, struggles with the complexities of family ties. The story examines the costs and compromises involved in striking a balance between the need of being present in one's loved ones' life and the unwavering pursuit of professional goals. This chapter explores the frailties of a guy who struggles with the universal difficulties of family relationships while controlling boardrooms and influencing industries.

Readers will watch Bryan Johnson's development as a business mogul and as a person looking for peace in a world where things are always changing as they turn the pages. The story explains the subtleties of decision-making, showing how the same visionary who plans business victories also navigates the complex web of family ties.

"Beyond Business" turns becomes a platform for examining the relationship between personal contentment and ambition. The chapter discusses Johnson's position as a father of three, the difficulties in juggling work and personal obligations, and the costs associated with pursuing greatness nonstop. The reader is faced with the heartbreaking reality that the inherent contradictions between professional objectives and the quieter yearnings of the heart exist even for giants of business.

This chapter's narrative crescendo is characterized by a deep reflection. Entrepreneur Johnson is troubled by issues of legacy, the mark he leaves on family ties, and the need to recalibrate in order to establish a healthy synthesis between his personal and professional lives. This chapter, in which the need for connection and authenticity is entwined with the quest of achievement, speaks to universal issues.

The reader is left with a complex picture of Bryan Johnson as "Chapter Two: Beyond Business" comes to an end. This includes his status as a tech icon as well as his humanity, as he must balance ambition and authenticity. In order to create a story that goes beyond the confines of business and speaks to a wider range of human experience, it explores the complex aspects of a life lived outside of boardrooms—a life where personal and professional goals meet.

Juggling Entrepreneurship and Love

This section of the biography offers an engrossing investigation of the beginnings of Johnson's romantic involvement with the well-known actress and content creator Taryn Southern. The story of Bryan Johnson's life takes a personal turn as we explore the subtopic of "Relationship Beginnings with Taryn Southern."

The chapter begins with their chance meeting, giving readers an insight into the chemistry of chance and connection that created the conditions for an intense romance. Johnson, who is well-known for his visionary endeavors in the technology sector, is presented in a new light as a man negotiating the turbulent waters of love. The story goes beyond boardrooms and into the emotional domain, presenting Johnson as a hero in the universal tale of human connection.

Readers will find themselves fully engrossed in the dynamics of their courtship as the pages turn—the shared moments, the developing intimacy, and the attraction that pulled them in closer. The story reveals the subtleties of their relationship, portraying a picture of two people figuring out the complexities of love against the backdrop of Johnson's lofty professional obligations.

Juggling Entrepreneurship and Love

In the subtopic "Balancing Love and Entrepreneurship," the theme of love is intricately interwoven with the overall story of entrepreneurship. This section provides readers with a nuanced examination of Johnson's attempt to balance the demands of a rapidly expanding business empire with the delicate nuances of sustaining a romantic partnership.

The chapter serves as a platform for analyzing the difficulties and successes that arise when love and business collide. Johnson, who is well-known for his skill in creating financial empires, shows up as a sympathetic character who struggles with the age-old problem of striking a balance between one's personal and professional goals.

Through the ups and downs of Johnson's relationship with Taryn Southern, readers are guided through the complexities of scheduling, the effects of high-stakes business decisions on interpersonal relationships, and the perseverance needed to maintain a relationship in the face of the fast-paced nature of entrepreneurial endeavors.

Readers will see how Johnson's understanding of the mutually beneficial relationship between love and entrepreneurship changes as the story progresses. This chapter explores the tactical adjustments, trade-offs, and epiphanies that occur when love turns from being a counterbalance to an inspiration that drives Johnson's journey into entrepreneurship.

This chapter, "Balancing Love and Entrepreneurship," highlights the universal truth that even in the middle of boardroom negotiations and strategic planning, the human heart yearns for equilibrium and authentic connection. It invites the reader to witness the vulnerability of a visionary entrepreneur who, despite scaling heights in the business realm, is confronted with the intrinsic complexities of maintaining a profound connection.

Together, the subtopics "Relationship Beginnings with Taryn Southern" and "Balancing Love and Entrepreneurship" create a story that goes beyond biography to provide readers with an understanding of

Bryan Johnson as a hero in the story of love and ambition. This is a story in which the path of a tech star and the journey of the heart combine to create a narrative that speaks to the universal dance of human experience.

Chapter 3: The Frontier of Neurotechnology and the Kernel

"Chapter Three: Kernel and the Neurotechnology Frontier" presents as a turning point in the story as Bryan Johnson's biography progresses, bringing readers into the intriguing nexus of science, invention, and the workings of the human brain.

This chapter begins with Johnson's exploration of the field of neurotechnology, which is a place where science fiction and reality collide. It also explains the origins of Kernel, an endeavor that goes beyond conventional tech environments and explores the mysterious domain of brain activity monitoring and cognitive enhancement.

The narrative invites readers into the imaginative world of Kernel, a company that Johnson founded in 2016. It reveals the goals and motives that led Johnson to devote not only his financial resources but also his intellectual energy to the neurotechnology frontier. Learning about Kernel is like embarking on an expedition into the unexplored domains of comprehending and enhancing the human brain.

Johnson's quest transcends business success, becoming a mission to unlock the mysteries of the mind and push the boundaries of human potential. As the pages unfold, the reader is introduced to the groundbreaking endeavors of Kernel, ranging from devices that measure electrical and hemodynamic signals produced by the brain to ambitious projects encompassing Alzheimer's disease, aging, concussions, meditation states, and strokes.

The chapter explores the difficulties Kernel faces, his partnerships with scientists, and the complex dance between scientific research and entrepreneurial aspirations. It also sheds light on Johnson's dual role as CEO and trailblazer in the field of neurotechnology, presenting him as a trailblazer forging ahead in unexplored scientific territory.

One of the most important aspects of "Chapter Three" is the examination of the ethical and societal ramifications of neurotechnology. The story raises issues related to privacy, cognitive enhancement, and the fine line that separates scientific advancement from moral obligation. Readers are left to wonder about the consequences of living in a society where brain activity is not only tracked but possibly enhanced.

Kernel's demonstration of helmet-like devices that can visualize and record brain activity signals the chapter's crescendo, and the implications for the ability of paralyzed people to communicate or for mental health patients to access new therapies are poignant with the altruistic undertones of Johnson's neurotechnology odyssey.

"Chapter Three: Kernel and the Neurotechnology Frontier" presents Johnson not only as an entrepreneur but also as a steward of technological advancement, balancing the careful balance between scientific curiosity and societal impact. It goes beyond the traditional bounds of a business biography, becoming a portal into a world where the frontiers of science intersect with the human quest for understanding and self-enhancement.

The story invites readers to reflect on the complex web of human cognition and the unwavering spirit of those who dare to venture into uncharted territory. As the chapter comes to an end, the reader is left with a deep appreciation for Johnson's bold vision and the possible knock-on effects of Kernel's endeavors on the future of neuroscience.

"Origins and Development of Kernel

Bryan Johnson's life story has an intriguing twist as we explore the subtopic of "Inception and Evolution of Kernel." This section unfolds as a crucial chapter that provides readers with a close examination of the origins and development of Kernel, an endeavor that ventures beyond conventional tech landscapes and into the mysterious field of neurotechnology.

The chapter begins with Kernel in the early phases of development, chronicling the beginnings of Johnson's idea to investigate the secrets of the human brain. The novel incubation phase, when goals emerge and ideas sprout, is introduced to the readers. Johnson's obsessive interest regarding the workings of the brain combined with his entrepreneurial zeal serves as the impetus for Kernel's creation.

The story reveals Kernel's evolutionary path as the pages flip. The reader follows the project's development from a theoretical seed of an idea to a real force pushing the boundaries of brain technology. In the cutthroat world of tech entrepreneurship, the chapter acts as a record of calculated risks, partnerships with bright scientists, and the fortitude needed to turn a concept into a real product.

The examination of Kernel's development creates a story with challenges and breakthrough moments threaded throughout. Johnson is shown as a visionary leader who successfully navigates the commercial strategy, team relationships, and social effect in addition to the technical difficulties of neurotechnology. The reader learns more about the complex position that Johnson plays—not only as a CEO but also as a trailblazer who helped to bring in a new age in the study of brain function.

Developing the Brain Monitoring of the Future

In the subtopic "Shaping the Future of Brain Monitoring," the theme of shaping the future is evident. Readers are invited to join Kernel on a visionary journey where she transcends the boundaries of conventional brain monitoring and becomes a signpost of revolutionary change in the field of neuroscience.

This chapter unfolds the technical innovations that Kernel spearheaded, from apparatuses that measure electrical and hemodynamic signals to large-scale initiatives that address aging, Alzheimer's illness, concussions, states of meditation, and strokes. Johnson's bold idea goes beyond just making money; it becomes a quest to transform brain imaging and uncover the possibility of cognitive improvement.

The social ramifications and moral dilemmas that Kernel's attempt to influence the direction of brain monitoring takes are all too clear to readers. The story raises important issues of responsibility that come with technological advancement, privacy, and the democratization of cognitive data. As he navigates the fine line between scientific advancement and social effect, Johnson not only establishes himself as a tech star but also as a custodian of ethical principles.

The reader is shown Kernel's presentation of helmet-like gadgets that can capture and visualize brain activity as the story builds to a crescendo. The ramifications of Johnson's neurotechnology odyssey's humanitarian undertones for people with mental health difficulties accessing new medications or paraplegic folks communicating are profound.

The narrative dyads "Inception and Evolution of Kernel" and "Shaping the

Future of Brain Monitoring" together go beyond the bounds of conventional biography. This is a story of scientific curiosity and entrepreneurial drive coming together to pave the way for a day when we may be able to monitor and perhaps improve the complexity of the human mind. This is a story that invites readers to reflect on the significant effects of Kernel's work on the changing field of neuroscience and the seemingly endless possibilities that lie ahead for technological advancement.

Chapter Four: Beyond Earth Ventures and the OS Fund

Within Bryan Johnson's extensive biography, "Chapter Four: OS Fund and Ventures Beyond Earth" is an engrossing story that goes beyond the typical confines of a corporate biography. This chapter invites readers to explore the exciting nexus of business, charity, and a forward-thinking search for endeavors that go beyond Earth.

The chapter begins with Johnson's conception of the OS Fund, a venture capital business, in October 2014. The OS Fund transforms into a channel for Johnson's dedication to promoting science and technology in unorthodox sectors, serving as more than merely an investment vehicle. Readers are welcome to explore the fund's strategic framework, which allocates $100 million of Johnson's own funds to support innovative projects.

The reader is exposed to the diverse range of projects supported by the OS Fund as the story progresses. These endeavors range from creating proteins that surpass the limitations of nature to creating kits that are able to identify illnesses via DNA analysis. The chapter turns into a creative mosaic that displays the bold initiatives of trailblazers inspired by Johnson's idea.

When the story shifts to initiatives that cross borders between landmasses, "Ventures Beyond Earth"'s thematic undertone becomes evident. Under Johnson's direction, the OS Fund starts to support initiatives that consider the potential for human extension beyond Earth. It turns into a story of business acumen interacting with humanity's larger desire to discover and colonize new lands.

The difficulties and successes of endeavors that stretch the bounds of conventional wisdom are fully experienced by readers. Johnson is shown to play the role of a venture catalyst—not only as an investor, but also as a visionary of a day when mankind would reach the stars. Johnson's daring to invest in both the idealistic future and the practical present is shown throughout the chapter.

"Chapter Four" culminates in a revelation that goes beyond technical advancements to represent the spirit of exploration and the unwavering human search for knowledge. The projects that the OS Fund supports grow into rays of optimism, illustrating the marriage of business with a more expansive plan for the future of humanity.

Readers are left with a deep admiration for Johnson's multifaceted approach to business as the chapter comes to an end. "OS Fund and Ventures Beyond Earth" is more than just an investment history; it's a story about a journey into the areas where commercial savvy meets a deep commitment to influencing the future—both here on Earth and beyond. It is evidence that, when driven by a visionary goal, entrepreneurship can go outside the box and open doors for projects that will reverberate through the innovation corridors for many years to come.

Establishing OS Fund and Its Purpose

This section becomes a focal point, giving readers an in-depth perspective on the origins and overarching mission of the OS Fund, a venture capital firm that transcends the traditional boundaries of investment by weaving together Johnson's visionary aspirations and commitment to advancing science and technology. The story of Bryan Johnson's life takes an intriguing turn in the exploration of this subtopic.

The story begins with the crucial event that occurred in October 2014 when Johnson established the OS Fund. Johnson had a strong conviction in the revolutionary potential of science and technology. The reader is introduced to the strategic foundations of this venture capital organization, which audaciously sets aside $100 million of Johnson's own funds to support businesses that dare to take risks. Rather than being a simple financial tool, the OS Fund represents Johnson's belief that meaningful projects should aim to develop humankind's technical capabilities rather than merely make a profit.

Readers are drawn into the purpose that drives the OS Fund as the story progresses. It turns into a channel for funding projects that push the envelope of what is considered feasible and that question the current quo. Johnson's bold goals for the OS Fund go beyond the conventional domains of technology to include endeavors that might revolutionize whole sectors, challenge established scientific theories, and advance humankind as a whole.

As the reader digs into Johnson's methodical process to selecting the OS Fund portfolio, the theme of mission-driven investing becomes evident. The mission encompasses a dedication to endeavors that are in line with the ethos of increasing human potential, resolving complicated challenges, and improving society, and goes beyond simple financial success.

Putting Money Into Emerging Technologies

The story flows naturally into the subtopic of "Investing in Future Technologies," where the reader is welcomed into the wide-ranging web of businesses that fall under the purview of the OS Fund. It becomes clear that Johnson has a different approach to investing than just looking for the next big cash opportunity. Instead, he deliberately seeks for business projects that have the potential to change the course of history.

The reader is presented to an array of endeavors supported by the OS Fund, ranging from creating proteins that overcome the limitations of nature to creating kits that can identify illnesses at the DNA level. Johnson's vision and faith in the ability of these technologies to bring about significant change are evident in the way each investment is approached like a strategic chess play.

The story highlights Johnson's function as a venture initiator. It soon becomes clear that his engagement entails more than just lending money; it also entails mentoring, strategic advice, and a forward-thinking perspective that extends beyond the near future. The businesses that make up the portfolio of the OS Fund are not only supported financially, but also collaborate with one another to further technical innovation.

Investing in future technologies has a theme that goes beyond the conventional boundaries of business biographies. It develops into a narrative thread that connects Johnson's business endeavors to the larger story of technological advancement. The businesses grow into innovation hotspots, demonstrating not just the savvy of their financiers but also their common goal of constructing a world in which technology is a force for good.

Readers are left with a deep respect for the OS Fund's goal as the chapter comes to an end. Not only is "Founding OS Fund and Its Mission - Investing in Future Technologies" a chapter in a biography, but it also serves as evidence of how visionary investment can help usher in a time when technology is used to transform society and unleash the full potential of humankind.

"Chapter Five: Blueprint - Chasing the Fountain of Youth"

This is a pivotal chapter that explores the introspective and individual search for eternal vitality in Bryan Johnson's captivating life story. This chapter presents an engrossing investigation of Johnson's bold attempt to challenge the traditional limitations of aging, providing readers with an insight into the complex fabric of his anti-aging campaign.

The beginning of the chapter introduces "Blueprint," a project that Johnson started in October 2021. This huge project becomes the focal point of the story, representing Johnson's unwavering quest to actively influence aging as well as comprehend it. The finer points of Blueprint, which aims to slow biological aging by carefully monitoring biomarkers and implementing customized health modifications, are open to readers.

The reader is drawn into Johnson's complex strategy for finding the spring of youth as the story progresses. Carefully monitoring biomarkers turns into a scientific quest that provides answers on the effects of customized health adjustments, such as taking more than 100 supplements a day. The chapter is transformed into a work of art using scientific research, biometric wearables, and a dedication to pushing the limits of what is thought to be achievable in the field of anti-aging.

As "Chasing the Fountain of Youth" dives into Johnson's individual experiences and insights, the chapter's overarching theme becomes apparent. Readers go on a trip that transcends scientific investigation and explores the domains of human development, rather than only being spectators. Johnson's open discussion of his anti-aging routine, which includes shockwave therapy and his search for a "18-year-old" erection, demonstrates the extent he is prepared to go in order to maintain his youthfulness.

The story delves into the wider field of anti-aging initiatives, illuminating the reality that Johnson is not the only one pursuing this goal. Alongside him on this voyage are the well-to-do, who substantially invest in health facilities and enterprises that promote rejuvenation. The chapter turns into a little version of a wider societal phenomena in which the desire for perpetual youth is not just a personal goal but also a shared aim.

Readers are presented with the conflicting views of Johnson's anti-aging attempts as the chapter goes on. Experts in aging-related professions criticize and doubt Johnson's efforts, but Johnson remains steadfast and believes his efforts have merit. The story turns into a sophisticated investigation of the meeting point of popular opinion and scientific aspirations.

"Blueprint - Chasing the Fountain of Youth" reaches a crescendo when Johnson says he can turn back the clock on his epigenetic age by 5.1 years. This discovery marks a turning point in both the story of Blueprint and the larger conversation on anti-aging. The reader is left with a mixture of feelings, including astonishment, skepticism, and intense curiosity about how such projects may affect human lifespan in the future.

The readers are left wondering about the consequences of Johnson's unrelenting pursuit as the chapter comes to an end. "Blueprint - Chasing the Fountain of Youth" is more than simply a biography; it's a monument to the human spirit's unwavering capacity to push limits, challenge the notion that aging is inevitable, and set out on a search for eternal life. The story turns into an examination of the age-old human quest to find the fabled fountain of youth, both as a scientific theory and as a profoundly intimate and life-changing experience.

"Revealing Project Blueprint"

The Anti-Aging Debate and Science"

The exploration of Bryan Johnson's complex story goes further with an examination of the subtopic "Unveiling Project Blueprint." This section provides an introduction to the origins of a project that has come to represent Johnson's unwavering efforts to thwart the aging process. The reveal turns into a symbolic curtain raise that lets readers inside the inner sanctuary of Blueprint's origins, goals, and guiding ideals that support this bold endeavor.

The beginning of the chapter reveals that Johnson's anti-aging journey reached a turning point when Project Blueprint was introduced in October 2021. The reader is led through the ideation stage and learns about the motivation behind this audacious project. As the name implies, the project turns into a blueprint—a painstakingly designed strategy meant to improve organ performance and health in order to reduce biological age.

Readers are engrossed in the complexities of Project Blueprint as the story progresses. The careful monitoring of biomarkers takes center stage, providing an insight into the level of scientific rigor involved in this undertaking. Johnson's dedication to improving organ health and function is evident as she spins a story that combines scientific research with a very emotional search for vitality.

"Unveiling Project Blueprint" has a deeper meaning than just an introduction. It turns into an exploration of the thoughts of an entrepreneur who views aging as an issue that has to be met head-on with scientific rigor rather than as something that is inevitable. A significant turning point in the story is reached when Project Blueprint is unveiled, turning it from a theoretical notion into a physical representation of Johnson's will to change the way people see aging.

The Anti-Aging Debate and Science

Parallel to the disclosure of Project Blueprint, the story takes an interesting turn with the subtopic "The Science and Controversy of Anti-Aging." This section develops into a sophisticated investigation of the larger context in which Johnson's anti-aging initiatives take place—a context marked by skepticism, scientific investigation, and a careful balancing act between ambition and controversy.

The reader is welcomed into the realm of scientific research on anti-aging, where

Johnson's quest is not just a personal one but also an attempt to push the limits of what is thought to be feasible. The chapter takes on the appearance of a painting, adorned with biomarkers, customized health modifications, and a daily intake of more than 100 supplements. The reader enters the role of a spectator in the scientific exploratory theater, seeing firsthand how cutting-edge science and the very personal quest for longevity meet.

But the disagreement casts a shadow as the story progresses. The chapter addresses the doubts and critiques of Johnson's anti-aging programs. Experts in aging-related professions cast doubt on the viability and effectiveness of such initiatives, adding another level of complexity to the story. The reader is forced to consider the conflict between the pursuit of science and the critical evaluation of doubters.

The examination of debate develops into a plot point that gives the tale more complexity. It explores the public conversation around Johnson's activities and highlights how scrutinizing criticism is a common part of the quest for perpetual youth. The chapter turns into a stage on which, against the background of public opinion, the drama of scientific aspiration plays out.

Readers leave "The Science and Controversy of Anti-Aging" with a deep respect for the complex dance between popular perception and scientific inquiry. It develops into a chapter that goes beyond the confines of a traditional biography, giving readers an up-close look at the intricate interactions between ambition, cynicism, and the enduring human desire to live a long life.

"Chapter Six: The Love Story Unraveled"

"Chapter Six: The Love Story Unraveled" in the engrossing biography of Bryan Johnson presents as a moving and complex investigation into the complexities of Johnson's love journey. This chapter acts as a turning point in the story, moving the emphasis from the high-stakes arena of entrepreneurship and anti-aging to the intimate realm of love and relationships and the enormous influence they have on a person's life.

As the chapter explores the intricacies of Johnson's love entanglements, the reader is brought into the world of his private encounters with ease. From the outside, the love story seems to be an ideal tale, but it unravels with a subtle reality that highlights the difficulties in striking a balance between personal relationships and the demands of a rigorous commercial goal.

The chapter reads like a tapestry, with strands of passion, dedication, and the unavoidable difficulties that arise when love and ambition collide. From the early phases of courting to the complexities of managing a relationship under the spotlight, readers are welcomed inside the private moments that shaped Johnson's personal journey.

The tale prompts reflection on the fine line that separates desires for both personal satisfaction and career success as the love story progresses. Johnson's experiences turn into a mirror that reflects the common obstacles that people who aspire to greatness in both their personal and public life must overcome. The chapter turns into a monument to the fragility that comes with following a vision that goes beyond accepted notions of what is possible.

"The Love Story Unraveled" explores the complex dance between love and ambition on a universal level, going beyond the specific experiences of its characters. It talks about the compromises, deep connections, and sacrifices that make up the human experience. The chapter creates empathy and understanding for the difficulties involved in pursuing both professional and personal satisfaction by acting as a bridge to link the reader with the private parts of Johnson's life.

The reader is made aware of the unavoidable flaws that characterize love tales as the story progresses. The unraveling takes on a symbolic quality as it moves away from romanticized ideas and toward a story that is more real and accessible. It turns into a chapter that speaks to everyone who has walked the complex path of love, ambition, and the search for a purposeful life in addition to those who are fascinated by Johnson's life.

Bryan Johnson's biography, "Chapter Six: The Love Story Unraveled," goes beyond the confines of a typical success story to provide readers an insight into the complexities, fragility, and sincerity that characterize the human experience. The reader may examine the complex interactions between intimate relationships and the unwavering pursuit of an extraordinary goal via the prism of the love tale.

"The Whirlwind Romance."

"The Whirlwind Romance" is a passionate, intense, and multifaceted chapter that comes to life in Bryan Johnson's convoluted life story. This passage acts as a literary doorway, bringing readers into the center of a love affair that happened as quickly and unpredictable as a storm. The chapter turns into a canvas on which the vibrant brushstrokes of passion depict a relationship marked by rapid development and deep connection.

The story begins with the beginning of Bryan and Taryn's relationship, which takes off on a fast-paced romance that defies expectations of time. Tracing the path of a relationship that blazed with an intensity that resembled the whirling winds of a storm, readers are engrossed in the heady mixture of emotions that accompany love at first sight. The chapter allows readers to experience the compelling attraction between two people engulfed in a fast-moving relationship that shattered preconceived ideas about courting in its wake.

Problems and Disputations in Taryn and Bryan's Relationship

As the story progresses, the focus moves to the difficulties and conflicts that surrounded Bryan and Taryn's relationship. The chapter delves into a comprehensive examination of the complications that often accompany public relationships, giving readers an insight into the dark side of the apparently perfect exterior of celebrity love.

The couple's struggles are used as a plot device to give the drama more depth. Readers are aware of the complexity of Bryan and Taryn's relationship, from the external factors driven by media attention to the internal tensions inherent in every close relationship. The chapter walks readers through the highs and lows, ebbs and flows, that come with a love story in the spotlight of public opinion.

As is inevitable for a love tale lived in the spotlight, controversy follows. The chapter turns into a venue for discussing how outside influences affect a relationship's complexities and illuminating the fine balance between an individual's right to privacy and the demands of public view. The conflicts serve as a prism through which readers may consider the difficulties people have while attempting to navigate love under the harsh glare of celebrity.

"The Whirlwind Romance: Challenges and Controversies in Bryan and Taryn's Relationship" becomes a chapter that goes beyond the bounds of a traditional love tale in the grand scheme of Bryan Johnson's history. It encourages readers to sympathize with the weaknesses revealed in the face of difficulties and controversies in addition to savoring the exhilarating highs of a flash romance. The narrative mosaic that emerges from the chapter embodies love in all of its turbulent splendor, prompting readers to consider the universal themes of passion, resiliency, and the complexities that characterize the human experience.

Chapter 7: Taryn Southern's Lawsuit and Legal Unrest

"Chapter Seven: Legal Turmoil - Taryn Southern's Lawsuit" is a crucial and dramatic chapter that plunges the story into the turbulent world of court cases and personal turmoil in Bryan Johnson's complex life story. This chapter turns into a courtroom drama, a real-life investigation of the complications that emerge when the harsh realities of litigation meet the private realm. A compelling story of conflict and resolve is told as the legal drama progresses, drawing readers into a web of intertwined love, ambition, and legal complexities.

The Dramatic Unveiling of Lawsuit

The unfolding of a legal drama that throws shadows on the narrative canvas opens the chapter. The lawsuit filed by Taryn Southern becomes a major narrative piece, adding suspense and doubt to the already gripping account of Johnson's life. The case threatens to upend Johnson's worldview, forcing him to face not just legal issues but also the complexities of intimate relationships in the spotlight. It is like a storm building on the horizon.

Legal Conflicts in the Public Eye

The story delves into the complexities of the litigation, analyzing the accusations, counterclaims, and the wider ramifications for both sides as the legal turbulence takes center stage. Through a voyage through courtrooms and legal documents, readers are guided through the intricate turns and turns of a legal war that goes beyond the typical bounds of commercial conflicts.

The chapter turns into a stage for legal drama, with real and legal people battling it out via words, papers, and public opinion.

Readers are given a front-row seat to the intricacies of high-stakes litigation, when reputations are at risk and the decisions made have far-reaching effects outside of the courtroom.

Effect in both the personal and professional spheres

The judicial unrest affects Bryan Johnson's personal and professional spheres in addition to the courtroom. The chapter turns into an analysis of the mutually reinforcing link between individual decisions and their legal implications. As Johnson attempts to preserve the delicate balance between his personal integrity, his professional reputation, and the demands of the legal system, his character is put to the test as he navigates the turbulent seas of legal disputes.

Thoughts on the Human Drama

The mirror image "Chapter Seven: Legal Turmoil - Taryn Southern's Lawsuit" highlights the human drama that accompanies court cases. It asks readers to consider the moral conundrums, psychological costs, and transforming effects that legal battles have on people and their relationships. The chapter turns into a literary furnace where people are put through their paces by intense legal examination, having their weaknesses revealed and their fortitude tried.

The biography travels beyond the conventional bounds of success tales in this chapter, delving into the complexities of the actual world. The legal turbulence turns into a metaphorical storm that sculpts Johnson's life, leaving readers hungry to find out about the conclusions, epiphanies, and fallout that will surely impact the next few chapters of this engrossing biography.

Johnson's Reaction and the Court Case

Summary of the Charges

This chapter opens with a thorough examination of the allegations, exposing the nuances of the claims that reverberate through the legal battleground. The narrative dramatically changes in this segment, diving into the center of the storm as the allegations against Bryan Johnson take center stage. Taryn Southern's lawsuit unfolds as a tapestry woven with accusations that send shockwaves through Johnson's personal and professional spheres.

The chapter painstakingly dissects the multifaceted claims that set the stage for a legal showdown. Readers are confronted with the stark realities of a high-profile legal battle, where personal grievances intertwine with financial ramifications, creating a narrative landscape rich in tension and uncertainty. The allegations span a spectrum of personal and professional dimensions, each thread adding layers of complexity to the unfolding drama.

Johnson's Reaction and the Court Case

Bryan Johnson's response becomes a crucial point in the developing drama, a skillfully crafted counterpoint to the allegations that seeks to defend his reputation and call into question the veracity of the claims; the legal battle becomes a battleground of words, documents, and strategic maneuvers, offering readers a ringside seat to the clash of legal titans. The chapter smoothly transitions into the intricate dance of legal proceedings as the allegations cast a shadow over Johnson's life.

Johnson's response is not just a legal defense but a narrative within the larger story—a story that transcends the boundaries of courtrooms and legal briefs, reaching into the core of human experience. The narrative examines the subtleties of Johnson's defense, breaking down the legal arguments, counterclaims, and the larger strategy employed to navigate the complexities of the lawsuit.

The Human Drama Starts

The chapter becomes a stage for the human drama inherent in legal disputes as the legal battle plays out; readers witness the toll that legal battles exact on individuals caught in their midst—decisions weighed with the gravity of potential consequences and the emotional strain of public scrutiny. Emotions run high as personal and professional reputations hang in the balance.

The courtroom becomes a theater where the human drama plays out, and the outcomes have far-reaching implications not only for the individuals involved but also for the narrative arc of Johnson's biography. Readers can contemplate the larger themes of justice, accountability, and the complexities that arise when personal and professional realms intersect through the lens of the legal proceedings.

The Challenging Journey Ahead

The chapter ends with readers feeling a sense of anticipation as they work through the summary of the allegations, Johnson's response, and the developing legal battle. The road ahead is unclear, and the resolution is still elusive. The legal drama serves as a catalyst for reflection, making readers consider the nature of justice, truth, and the fortitude of people who must face the difficult obstacles of a legal storm.

This section of the biography goes beyond the conventional bounds of success stories and explores the unexplored realm of legal complexities. The accusations, Johnson's response, and the legal battle together constitute a narrative triad that beckons readers to embark on an adventure that surpasses the surface level of success and provides an insight into the complex dance of interpersonal relationships, legal complexities, and the capricious turns that characterize the remaining chapters in Bryan Johnson's extraordinary life.

Chapter 8: Bryan's Personal and Professional Struggles - Life's Complicated ornament

"Chapter Eight: Life's Complex Tapestry" is a moving examination of the complex interactions between personal and professional struggles that form the very fabric of Bryan Johnson's life, as the story of his life gradually comes to light. This chapter dives deeply into the complexities of Johnson's journey, weaving together threads of triumphs and tribulations, successes and setbacks, revealing the raw and unfiltered portrait of a man navigating the maze of life's challenges.

Handling Your Own Personal Chaos

Beginning with a close examination of Johnson's personal struggles, the chapter reveals vulnerabilities hidden beneath the surface of success. Readers are invited into the inner sanctum of Johnson's emotions as he describes the dynamics of his family, relationships, and the profound effects of his choices on his life's tapestry. The story is transformed into a canvas on which emotions are delicately painted, capturing the highs and lows of Johnson's journey.

The Peer Pressure of Career Goals

The chapter lays bare the complexities of building and sustaining empires, exploring the price extracted by the relentless pursuit of success. As the story progresses, the focus moves to the professional realm, where Johnson struggles with the formidable challenges that come with being an entrepreneur. Readers witness the juggling act required to balance visionary aspirations with the day-to-day demands of business, as Johnson confronts the inherent tensions woven into the fabric of entrepreneurial life.

Achievements and Failures: A Parallel Story

The story of "Life's Complex Tapestry" is told in two parts, with the successes and failures that mark Johnson's journey alternately highlighted and subdued. Success stories shine a bright light on the chapter, but are always accompanied by the shadows of inescapable difficulties. From the pinnacle of personal hardships to the height of entrepreneurial accomplishments, readers are taken on an exhilarating journey through the highs and lows that characterize Johnson's complex life.

Striking a Balance: Managing Two Worlds

A meditation on the inherent tension between personal happiness and the unwavering drive for success, this chapter centers on the exploration of the delicate balance Johnson must strike between personal fulfillment and professional pursuits. Johnson's struggles become representative of the larger human experience, as readers face the universal challenge of navigating the complex dance between personal contentment and professional ambitions.

Thoughts on the Human Situation

"Chapter Eight: Life's Complex Tapestry" defies classification as a traditional biography and instead becomes a meditation on the larger human condition. Johnson's journey serves as a mirror for readers to reflect on their own challenges, goals, and the fragile fabric of life. The chapter encourages readers to reflect on the nature of success, the real cost of ambition, and the resiliency needed to deal with life's obstacles.

In this section of Johnson's biography, the story transcends from being a simple record of successes and failures to a multifaceted tapestry intertwined with human experiences, providing readers with a deep and contemplative look into the complex tapestry of a life lived at the crossroads of personal and professional goals.

Managing Divorce and Quitting the Mormon Church

This chapter in Bryan Johnson's life is a powerful story of perseverance, change, and the lasting effects of important life choices. The first section of the chapter delves into Johnson's own experience of adjusting to divorce, highlighting the emotional complexities involved in ending a meaningful relationship. As Johnson navigates the turbulent seas of separation, readers are taken into the depths of his emotions as he considers the reflection and personal development that often follow such life-altering occurrences.

The story goes into further detail on Johnson's split from the LDS Church (the Church of Jesus Christ of Latter-day Saints). As Johnson struggles with issues of identity, religion, and the significant ramifications of leaving the theological basis that previously formed his worldview, this spiritual journey turns into a furnace of self-discovery. As they follow Johnson's spiritual journey, readers have a better understanding of the internal struggles and outside obstacles that come with such significant changes.

Health Plans and Intense Wellness Objectives

The chapter deftly switches from discussing personal turmoil to examining Johnson's dedication to rigorous wellness initiatives and health routines. In his pursuit of optimum well-being, Johnson becomes a leader in the field of biohacking, which is open to readers. The story is woven together by scientific investigation, careful biomarker monitoring, and the unwavering quest for physical health.

The examination of extreme wellness endeavors offers readers an insight into Johnson's commitment to exploring the limits of human potential. Johnson's approach to well-being, which incorporates over 100 supplements everyday and involves intricate dietary habits like intermittent fasting and calorie restriction, is a monument to the convergence of science and individual willpower.

A Harmony of Change

In Johnson's life, the contrast of going through a divorce, leaving the LDS Church, and pursuing extreme health activities produces a symphony of change. The chapter turns into a comparison study that shows how spiritual, physical, and personal elements are all intertwined. Readers follow Johnson's transformation, a journey that goes beyond the physical to explore the depths of the human soul.

Through this story, Johnson's life is transformed into a canvas on which the qualities of curiosity, resilience, and an unwavering quest for personal growth collide. The chapter invites readers to consider the complex relationship that exists between the decisions we make in response to life's obstacles. Johnson's story serves as an inspirational example of the transformational potential that arises from intentionally managing hardship, accepting change, and blazing a trail towards holistic well-being.

"Coping with Divorce and Leaving the LDS Church, Health Regimens and Extreme Wellness Pursuits" is essentially a chapter that captures the essence of Johnson's complex journey, which is characterized by significant life decisions, spiritual development, and an unwavering dedication to expanding the definition of what it means to live an optimal and purposeful life.

"Chapter Nine: Writing a New Chapter on Children's Books and Creative Pursuits

"Chapter Nine: Writing a New Chapter" in Bryan Johnson's life story is a vivid look at the relationship between creativity, parenting, and the limitless possibilities of the imagination. This chapter explores Johnson's path into children's literature and creative endeavors, shedding light on a side of his experiences where narrative serves as a vehicle for inspiration, knowledge, and the joyful investigation of the human spirit.

The Origins of Artistic Expression

The beginning of the chapter presents a clear picture of how Johnson first used children's books as a vehicle for his creative expression. Readers are drawn into the narrative process, where Johnson's inventiveness is shown. The story takes shape as a literary tapestry woven with imagination, wonder, and a deep comprehension of the enchantment that captivates young minds.

Cracking the Code for an Epic Life in Code 7

One of the main topics of discussion in this chapter is Johnson's foray into children's books with the release of "Code 7: Cracking the Code for an Epic Life." The story draws readers into the magical universe that Johnson creates, one in which young readers take an active role in the quest to unlock life's codes rather than being passive spectators. The chapter develops as an ode to the ability of literature to uplift, instruct, and arouse awe in the hearts of future generations.

The Proto Project: A Mental Science Fiction Journey

The examination of Johnson's artistic endeavors continues with "The Proto Project: A Sci-Fi Adventure of the Mind." This book demonstrates the author's flexibility as it moves from the self-help genre to the captivating science fiction genre. The story opens up a world where the imagination is limitless, beckoning readers of all ages to go off on an adventure beyond the confines of reality.

Raising Children and the Craft of Narrative

"Writing a New Chapter" offers readers an intimate look at the relationship between storytelling and parenting that goes beyond the boundaries of conventional biographical narrative. Parenting gets entwined with

Johnson's artistic endeavors, weaving a tale in which the pleasures and difficulties of parenting coexist peacefully with the fantastical worlds he creates in his novels.

Literary Legacy Contribution

The events of this chapter contribute to Johnson's literary heritage, which transcends the boundaries of commercial acumen and delves into the ageless art of narrative. The story turns into an ode to Johnson's dedication to making a lasting impression on the literary world—one that reaches beyond the boundaries of commercial success and into the hearts and minds of readers of all ages.

"Chapter Nine: Writing a New Chapter" is essentially a celebration of the storytelling medium's transforming potential and the art form's seamless incorporation into the fabric of a complex existence. The chapter encourages readers to rediscover the power of storytelling and the lasting influence it may have on molding hearts, minds, and the eternal legacy of a life well-lived via Johnson's foray into children's literature and creative expression.

This part of Bryan Johnson's story is an engrossing investigation into the two domains of financial savvy and artistic expression. A testimony to Johnson's complex personality, "Literary Pursuits" shows how the businessman skillfully combines the craft of storytelling with his commercial endeavors, making a lasting impression on both the literary and corporate worlds.

The Creative Imagination Meets the Entrepreneurial Spirit

The chapter begins with a detailed examination of Johnson's spirit of entrepreneurship and how it works in tandem with his imaginative creativity. The dynamic area where the demands of business and the limitless domains of creativity collide is extended to the readers. Johnson's path becomes an example of the transformational potential of embracing multiple interests as it becomes a study in the peaceful coexistence of apparently incompatible endeavors.

"Code 7": Unlocking the Secret to an Outstanding Life

This chapter devotes a good deal of attention to Johnson's first book, "Code 7: Cracking the Code for an Epic Life." It explores the origins of this children's self-help treasure. Johnson's desire to use compelling stories to teach important life lessons is evident, drawing readers into a universe where storytelling serves as a means of empowering the next generation. In addition to being a work of literature, "Code 7) demonstrates Johnson's dedication to forming young people's brains and giving them a sense of direction.

"The Proto Project": A Mental Sci-Fi Adventure

This investigation continues with Johnson's science fiction project, "The Proto Project: A Sci-Fi Adventure of the Mind." The tale reveals an area where Johnson's inventiveness transcends the conventions of traditional storytelling. A tribute to Johnson's ability as a writer, "The Proto Project" skillfully traverses a variety of genres and captivates readers with stories that go beyond the norm. This venture into science fiction adds a new facet to Johnson's creative toolbox and demonstrates his determination to go into unexplored literary realms.

Handling the Interaction Between Creativity and Business

The chapter deftly handles the interaction between Johnson's contributions to the arts and his financial endeavors. Readers learn how Johnson, who is well-known for his achievements in the business world, easily directs his imagination into writing projects. The story turns into an inventive and balanced study, demonstrating Johnson's skill at negotiating the complexities of both boardrooms and creative environments.

Effects on Legacy, Both Personal and Professional

"Literary Pursuits" closes with a consideration of the enduring influence of Johnson's artistic endeavors on his legacy, both personally and professionally. Johnson's story is distinguished by the way in which financial success and literary pursuits come together, highlighting the idea that genuine innovation often results from the blending of disparate interests. Johnson makes a lasting impression on the literary world with "Code 7" and "The Proto Project," encouraging readers to consider the relationship between creativity and enterprise.

"Literary Pursuits: 'Code 7' and 'The Proto Project' - Creative Contributions Amidst Business Ventures" is essentially a chapter in which Johnson's rich activities outside of the boardroom are celebrated. It encourages readers to see the skillful blending of creative imagination with commercial savvy, reiterating the notion that genuine innovation is boundless and may appear at the most unexpected intersections.

"Chapter Ten: Legacy and Reflections".

In "Chapter Ten: Legacy and Reflections," the last chapter of Bryan Johnson's gripping story, readers are taken on a contemplative journey through the fabric of a life well lived, reflecting on the enduring legacy forged through entrepreneurship, creativity, and the unwavering pursuit of innovation. This chapter offers a moving perspective on the terrain of Johnson's accomplishments, obstacles, and the lasting impact he has on the fields of business, literature, and the very definition of what it is to pursue a lasting legacy.

Reflective Moments

The chapter begins with retrospective looks at significant turning points and life events that have influenced Johnson's path. Readers are encouraged to relive the origins of entrepreneurship, the journey of creativity via children's books, and the bold pursuit of anti-aging projects. These glimpses provide a comprehensive picture of a life that defies easy classification, exposing a man whose influence is felt in many different domains, all of which add to the complex mosaic of his global influence.

The Meeting Point of Creativity and Business

The interaction between Johnson's business sense and his artistic endeavors is a major subject in this chapter. The story offers insights into how Johnson's spirit of entrepreneurship coexists harmoniously with his ventures into the fields of neurology, literature, and cutting-edge anti-aging technology. The convergence of these apparently unrelated endeavors serves as evidence of Johnson's comprehensive approach to creating a legacy that cuts across traditional lines.

The Textual Trace

Within this chapter, "Literary Pursuits: 'Code 7' and 'The Proto Project'" are explored, highlighting the long-lasting influence of Johnson's contributions to childhood reading. A key component of his literary legacy is the investigation of storytelling as a means of empowering people and stimulating their creativity. The chapter explores Johnson's stories' significance, looking at how they still influence young people's thinking and add to a larger cultural narrative.

Odyssey Against Aging and Project Blueprint

The chapter reads like a thoughtful investigation of Johnson's bold search for anti-aging technology. The outline of "Project Blueprint" is reexamined, providing new light on the debates, achievements, and wider ramifications of an endeavor to overcome the traditional limitations of aging. Johnson's thoughts on the importance of this undertaking take center stage, provoking readers to consider the limits of human possibility and the unwavering quest for a revitalized life.

Evolution of the Self and the Profession

"Legacy and Reflections" takes viewers on a journey through Bryan Johnson's subtle personal development in addition to his outward achievements. The chapter develops as a blank canvas on which the lessons learned from a life full of varied experiences, personal development, and fortitude in the face of adversity are all revealed. Johnson's observations serve as a guide for readers as they traverse their own paths, imparting wisdom on persistence, flexibility, and the everlasting need of accepting one's own personality.

Effects on Upcoming Generations

The latter sections of this chapter consider how Bryan Johnson's legacy will affect future generations. Readers are challenged to think about the broad ramifications of a life devoted to breaking down barriers, encouraging innovation, and redefining the possibilities both within and outside of the economic and literary domains. Johnson's legacy serves as both an encouragement to others to start their own innovative and self-discovery adventures and a monument to his own accomplishment.

"Chapter Ten: Legacy and Reflections" is essentially a moving conclusion to Bryan Johnson's life story. It goes beyond what may be considered a traditional biography and invites readers to reflect on the lasting impact of a life lived with passion, purpose, and an unflinching devotion to leave a legacy that reverberates through the ages

Concluding the Excursion: The Unresolved Pursuit of Eternal Youth

This chapter captures the essence of Bryan Johnson's narrative, giving readers a panoramic view of the triumphs, challenges, and lingering echoes of an unfinished quest for timeless youth. As we draw the final curtain on the exploration of his multifaceted life, the conclusion serves as a reflective pause—a moment to synthesize the myriad threads that weave together the tapestry of his extraordinary journey.

Thinking Back on Successes and Difficulties

The book ends with a thoughtful analysis of the victories that have dotted Johnson's path. From the explosive growth and strategic acquisitions of Braintree to the ground-breaking projects like Kernel and OS Fund, readers are guided through the landscape of accomplishments that characterize Johnson's legacy. The story uncovers the critical junctures at which Johnson's vision came to pass and produced revolutionary contributions to the fields of technology, neuroscience, and venture capital.

But intertwined throughout the fabric are the strands of difficulties—personal, professional, and ethical. The story tackles the controversy surrounding Project Blueprint and the legal turbulence sparked by Taryn Southern's lawsuit. It explores the difficulties of juggling personal relationships with the demanding world of entrepreneurship, offering a complex portrait of a life full of both genius and complexity.

The Unresolved Search for Eternal Youth

The theme of Johnson's search for eternal youth runs through the conclusion. Project Blueprint, with its daring attempts to stop aging, is explored as a representation of human tenacity and the unwavering search for the unknown. The chapter explores the debates surrounding anti-aging treatments, providing a fair analysis of the goals of science and the responses of society to Johnson's audacious endeavor.

This chapter serves as a catalyst for reflection, asking readers to consider the implications of humanity's unrelenting quest for immortality. It acknowledges that the quest for timeless youth is still unfinished— an ongoing odyssey marked by scientific curiosity, unexplored territories, and the unwavering spirit of a visionary. Readers are invited to wrestle with the profound questions posed by Johnson's pursuits: Can we transcend the boundaries of aging, and at what cost? What ethical considerations accompany the pursuit of radical longevity?

The Past and the Future

This chapter examines how Johnson's legacy transcends boardrooms and laboratories, shaping the discourse on the intersection of humanity, technology, and the pursuit of a better future. As the story draws to a close, it widens its lens to encompass Johnson's legacy and the horizons that stretch beyond the present. The investigation of his impact on technology and science underscores the enduring influence of a mind that dared to envision possibilities beyond conventional limits.

Its epilogue and final pages serve as both a prologue to the unwritten stories yet to be written and a reflection on the unfolding chapters of Johnson's life. The epilogue and final pages ring with a sense of continuity—an acknowledgment that the chapters explored in this biography are not endpoints but chapters in an ongoing narrative.

"Conclusion: Summing Up the Journey - The Unfinished Quest for Timeless Youth" is, in essence, an invitation to embrace the never-ending voyage of discovery, creativity, and the continuing desire for a timeless, young spirit rather than just bidding adieu to the pages flipped.

Made in the USA
Las Vegas, NV
12 January 2025

16246490R00066